SandCastle™

Baby
African Animals

It's a Baby Chimpanzee!

Kelly Doudna

Consulting Editor, Diane Craig, M.A./Reading Specialist

ABDO
Publishing Company

Published by ABDO Publishing Company, 8000 West 78th Street, Edina, Minnesota 55439.

Printed in the United States.

Editor: Liz Salzmann
Content Developer: Nancy Tuminelly
Cover and Interior Design and Production: Mighty Media
Photo Credits: Digital Vision, iStockPhoto (Peter Malsbury), Peter Arnold Inc. (Michel Gunther, C. Huetter, Stéphanie Meng, P. Oxford, Cyril Ruoso, A. Shah)

Library of Congress Cataloging-in-Publication Data

Doudna, Kelly, 1963-
  It's a baby chimpanzee! / Kelly Doudna.
    p. cm. -- (Baby African animals)
  ISBN 978-1-60453-152-7
1. Chimpanzees--Infancy--Juvenile literature. I. Title.

QL737.P96D68 2009
599.885'139--dc22
                          2008005469

SandCastle™ Level: Fluent

SandCastle™ books are created by a team of professional educators, reading specialists, and content developers around five essential components—phonemic awareness, phonics, vocabulary, text comprehension, and fluency—to assist young readers as they develop reading skills and strategies and increase their general knowledge. All books are written, reviewed, and leveled for guided reading, early reading intervention, and Accelerated Reader® programs for use in shared, guided, and independent reading and writing activities to support a balanced approach to literacy instruction. The SandCastle™ series has four levels that correspond to early literacy development. The levels are provided to help teachers and parents select appropriate books for young readers.

Emerging Readers
(no flags)

Beginning Readers
(1 flag)

Transitional Readers
(2 flags)

Fluent Readers
(3 flags)

SandCastle™ would like to hear from you. Please send us your comments and suggestions.
sandcastle@abdopublishing.com

Vital Statistics

for the Chimpanzee

BABY NAME
there is no special name

NUMBER IN LITTER
1

WEIGHT AT BIRTH
4 pounds

AGE OF INDEPENDENCE
7 to 11 years

ADULT WEIGHT
70 to 120 pounds

LIFE EXPECTANCY
45 to 50 years

Chimpanzees are born completely helpless.

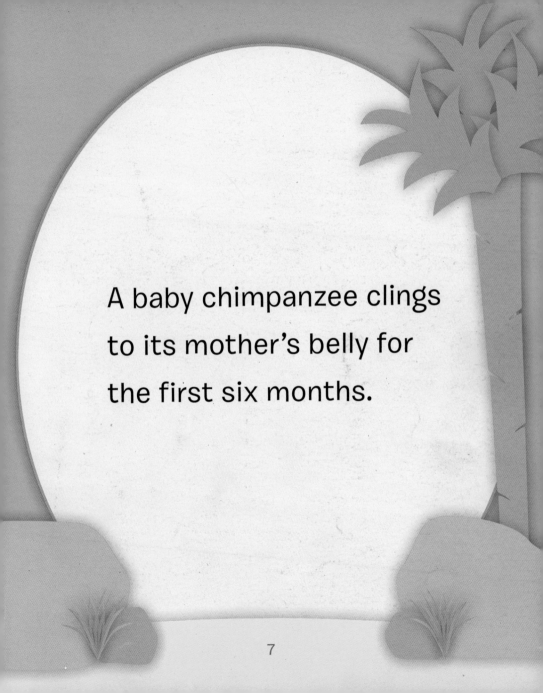

A baby chimpanzee clings to its mother's belly for the first six months.

Chimpanzees live in family groups that have six to ten members. Several family groups live together in a community.

Baby chimpanzees have a white tail tuft. This disappears as they age.

A male chimpanzee doesn't help raise his offspring. But he does help defend the territory of his family's community.

Leopards are the main animal predator of young chimpanzees.

Chimpanzees are omnivores. They eat mostly leaves, fruit, and insects.

Chimpanzees live in tropical forests and wet savannas.

Chimpanzees live in areas that have a lot of fruit trees.

Chimpanzees are very social. They use many different vocal sounds to communicate. They also drum on trees.

Chimpanzees form social bonds by grooming each other.

Male chimpanzees stay
with their family group.
Young females usually find
a new community to join.

Fun Fact

About the Chimpanzee

Other than humans, chimpanzees are one of only a few animals that use tools. They use sticks to dig for insects. They use rocks to smash nuts.

Glossary

communicate – to share ideas, information, or feelings.

expectancy – an expected or likely amount.

groom – to clean the fur of an animal.

independence – no longer needing others to care for or support you.

offspring – the baby or babies of an animal.

omnivore – one who eats both meat and plants.

predator – an animal that hunts others.

savanna – a grassland with few trees.

social – enjoying the company of others.

territory – an area that is occupied and defended by an animal or a group of animals.

tropical – located in the hottest areas on earth.

tuft – a short cluster of hairs or feathers.

To see a complete list of SandCastle™ books and other nonfiction titles from ABDO Publishing Company, visit **www.abdopublishing.com**.

8000 West 78th Street, Edina, MN 55439

800-800-1312 • 952-831-1632 fax